EXTREME DOT PUZZLES WITH OVER 15000 DOTS

DOT TO DOT PUZZLE

BY **MODERN PUZZLES PRESS**

MASTERPIECES OF ART

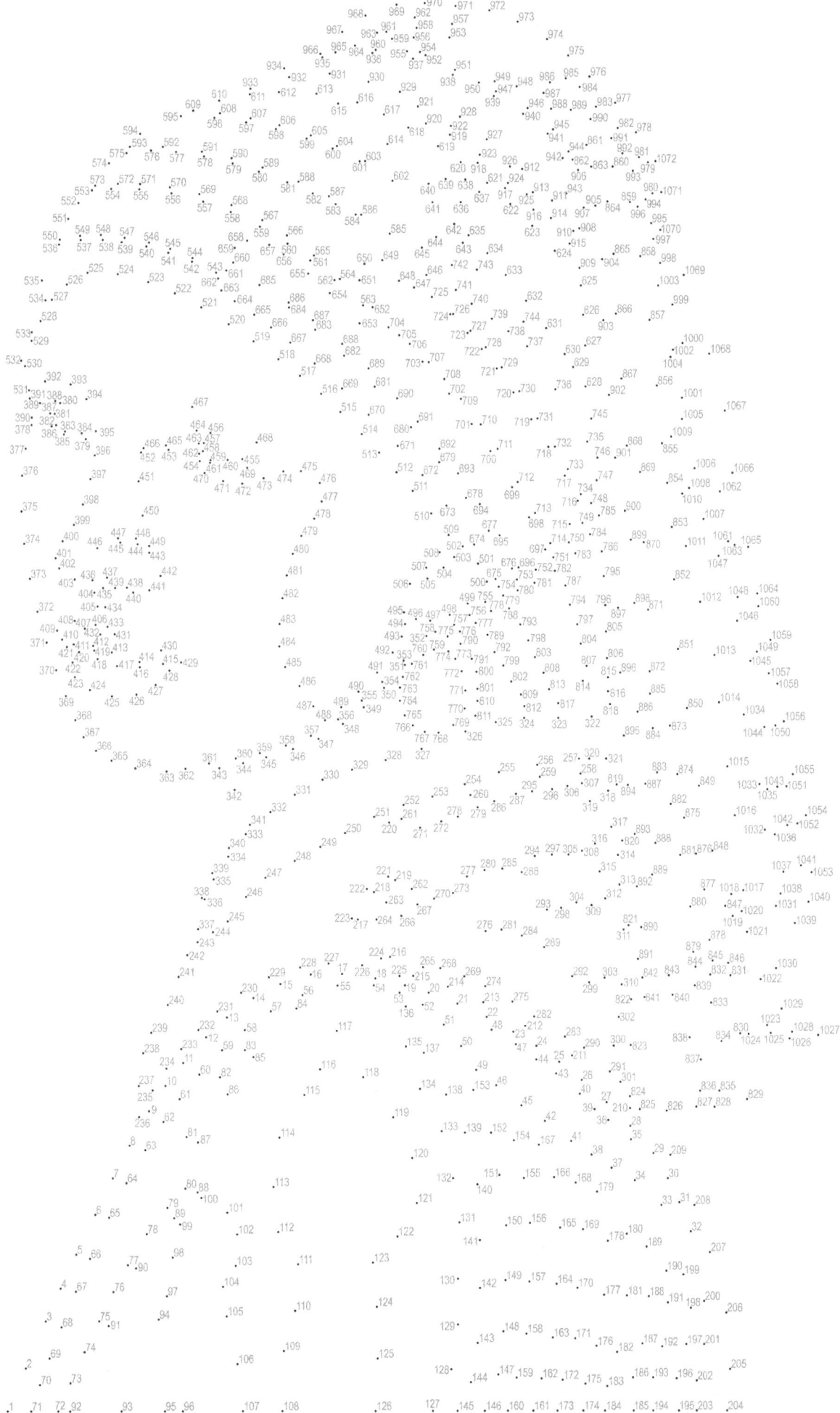

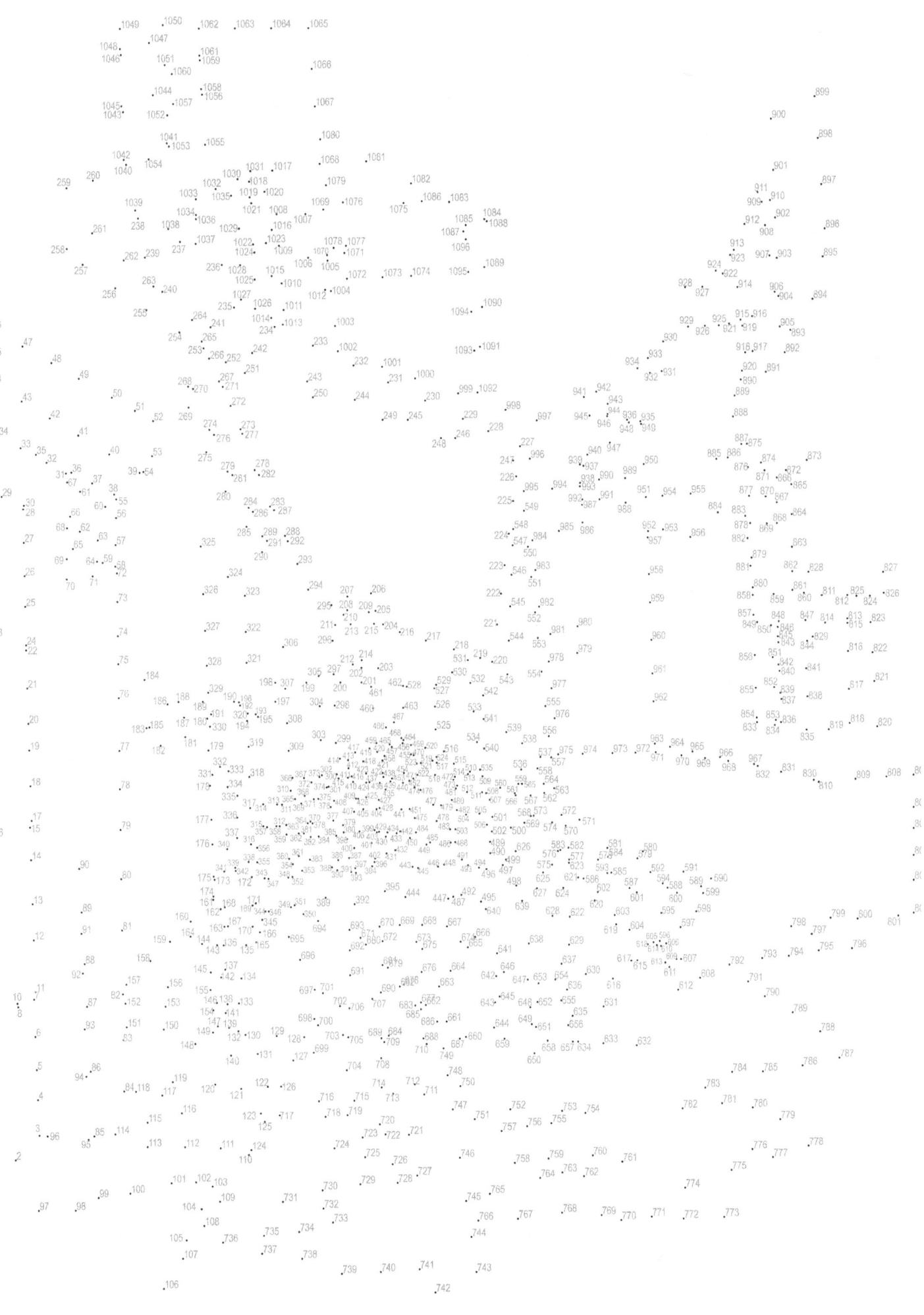

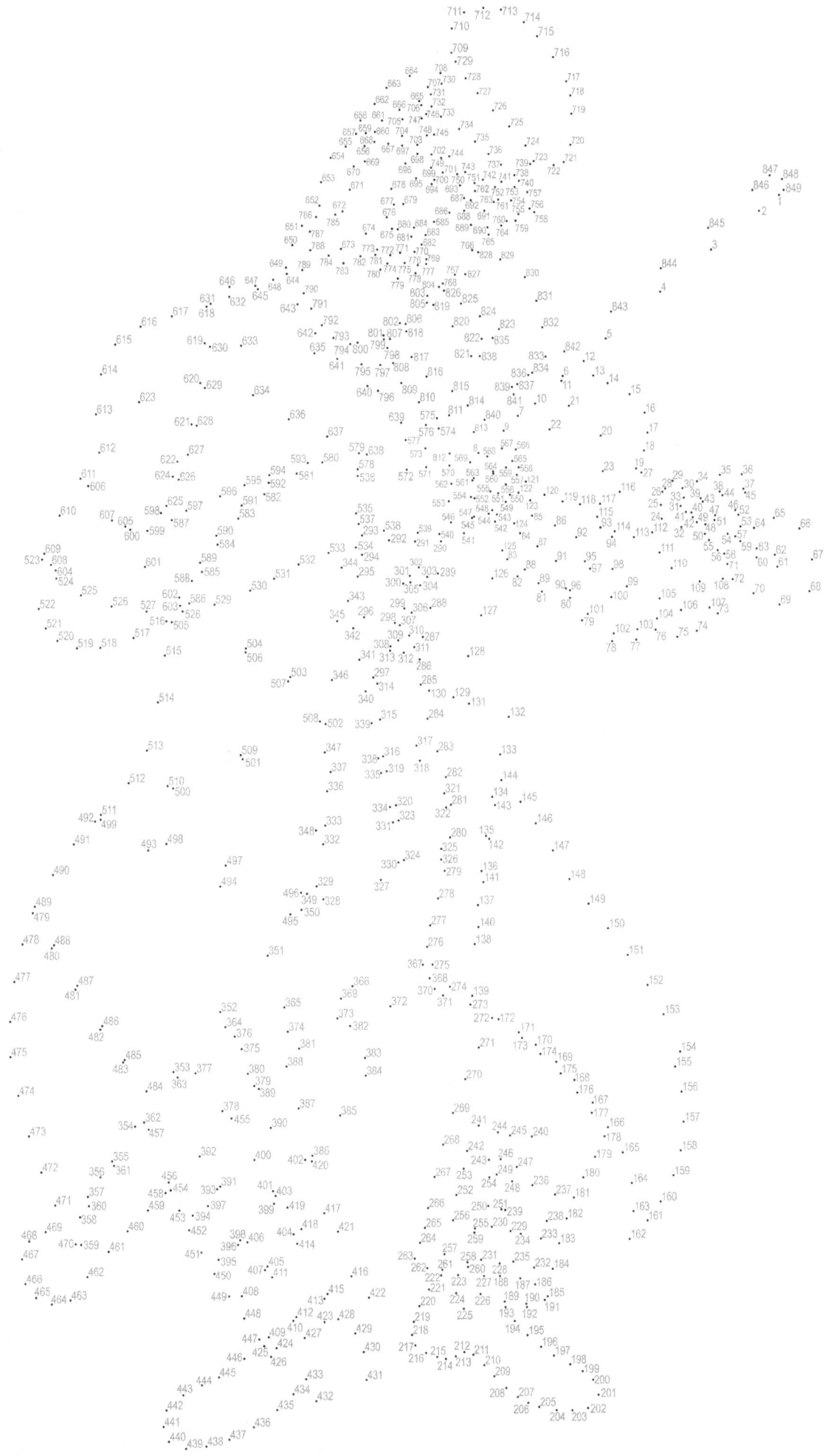

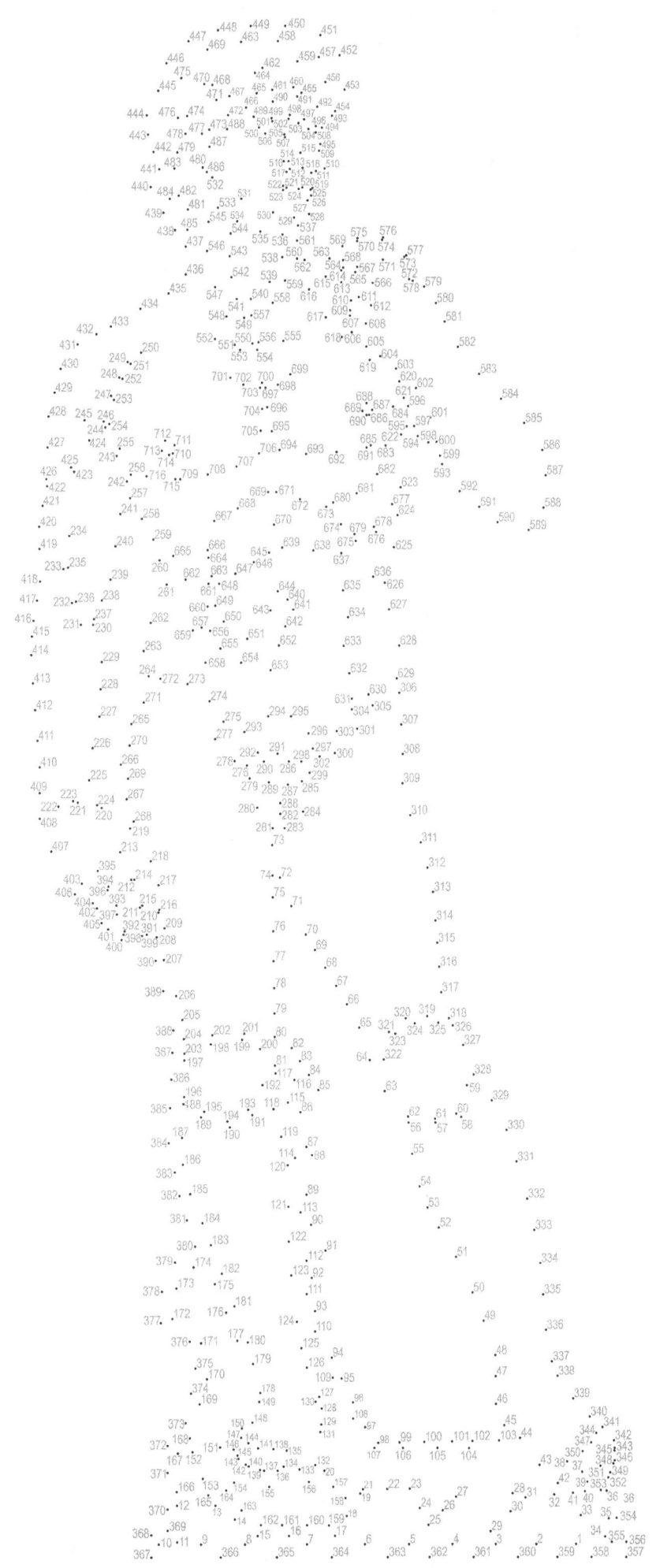

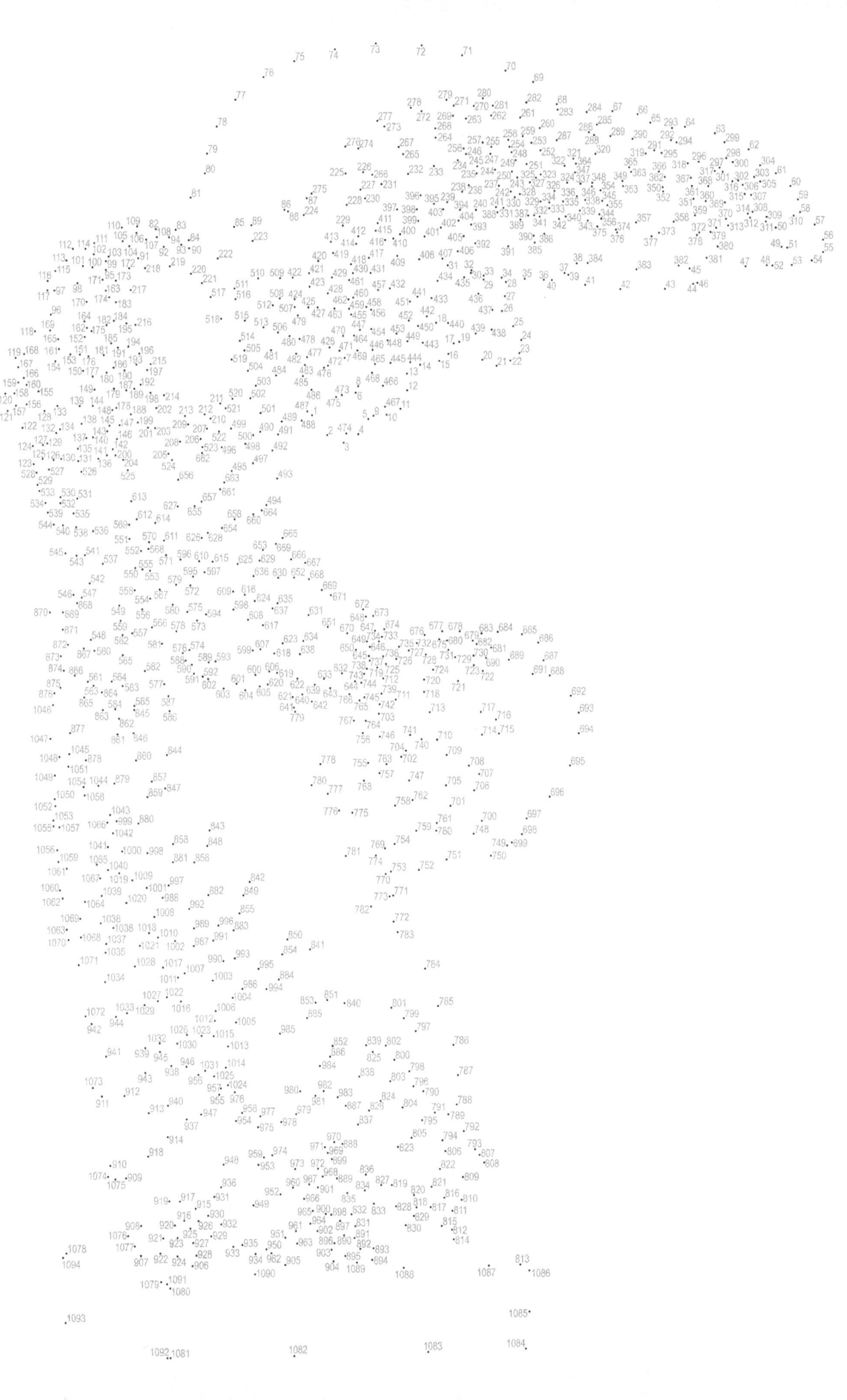

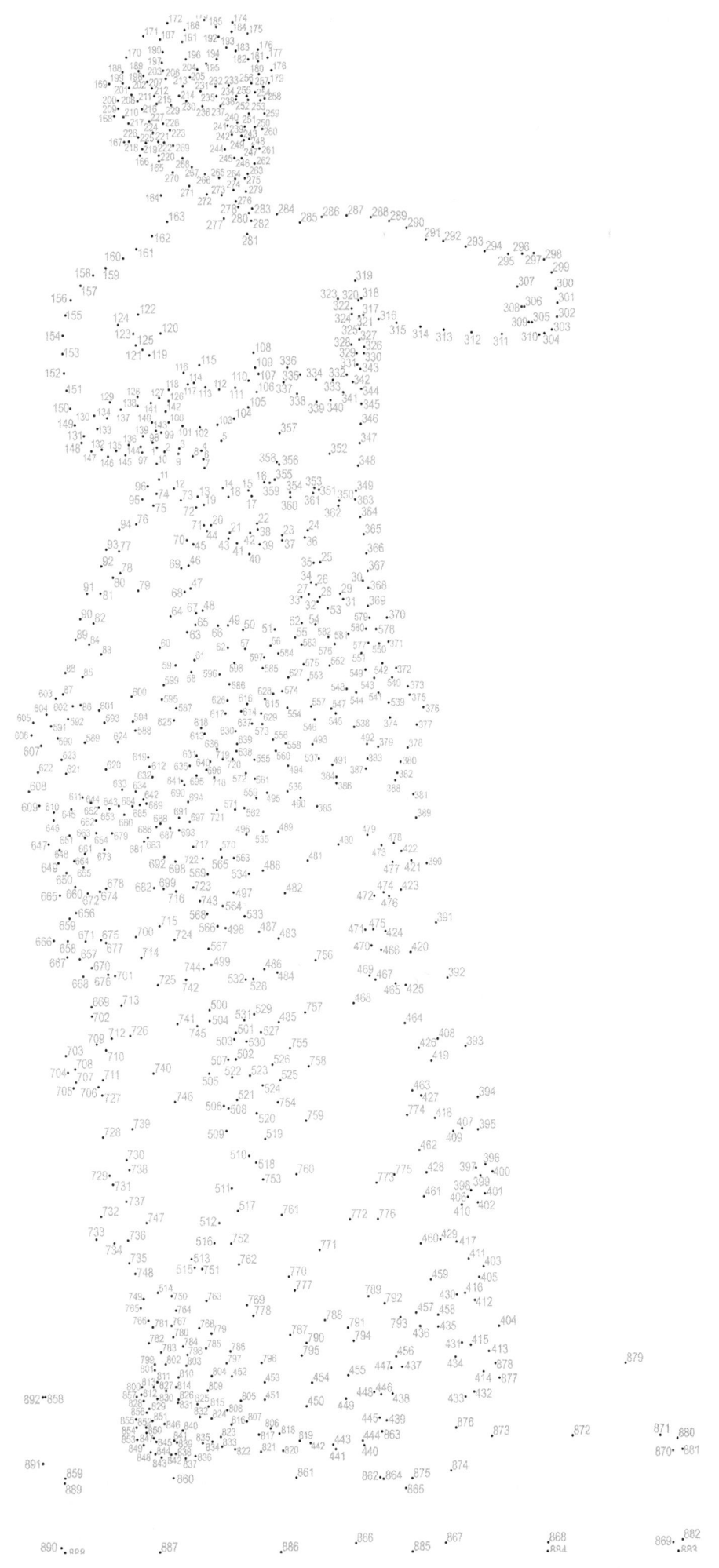

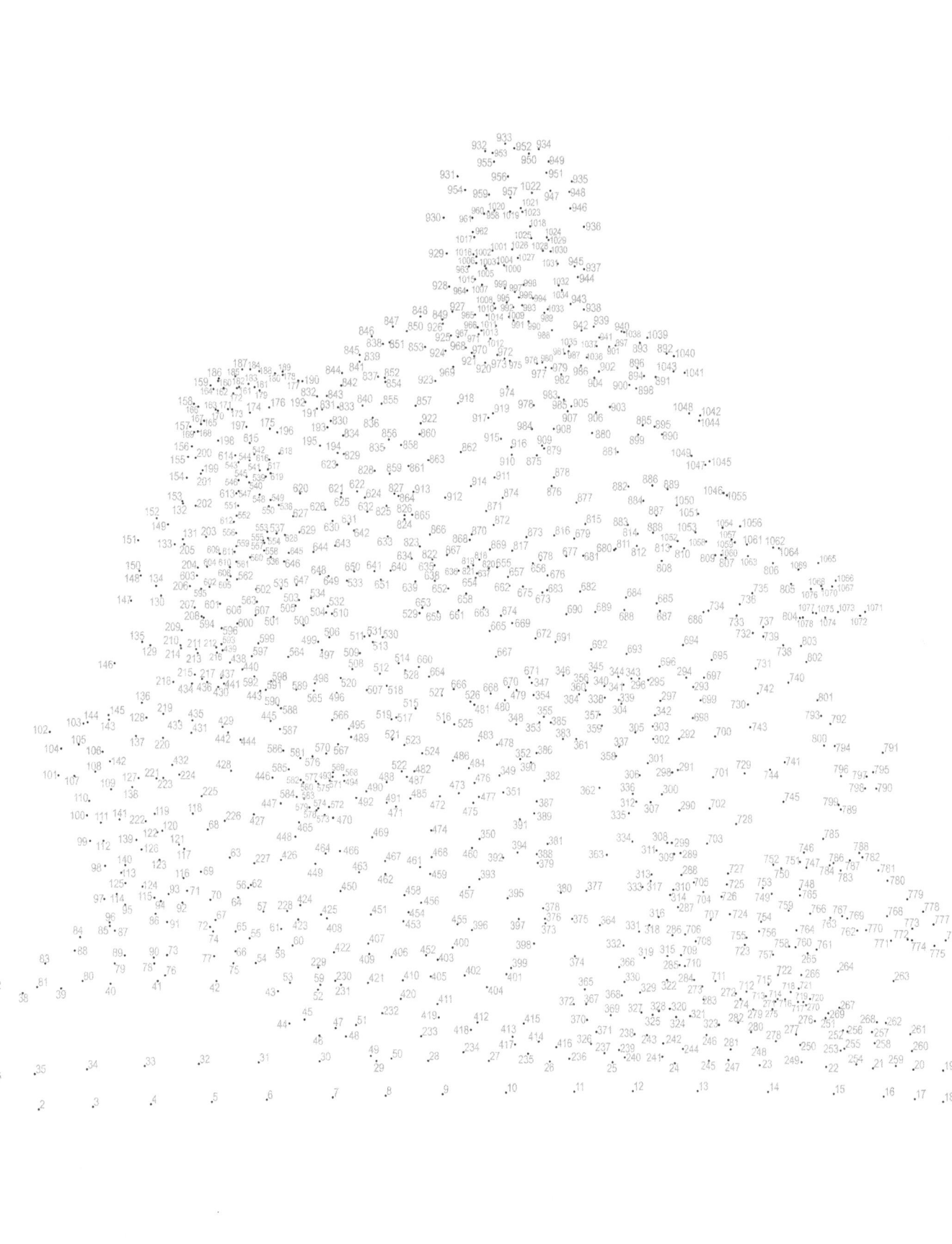

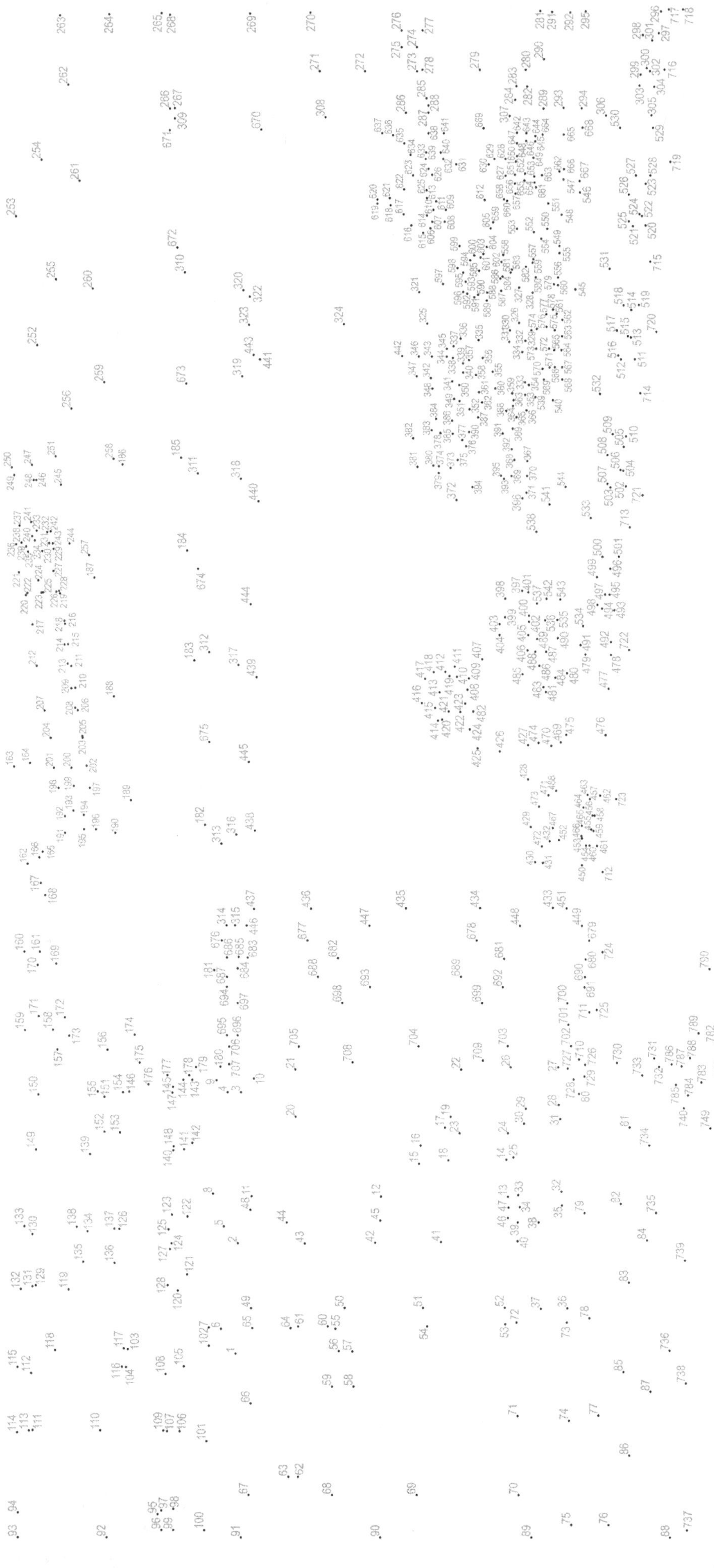

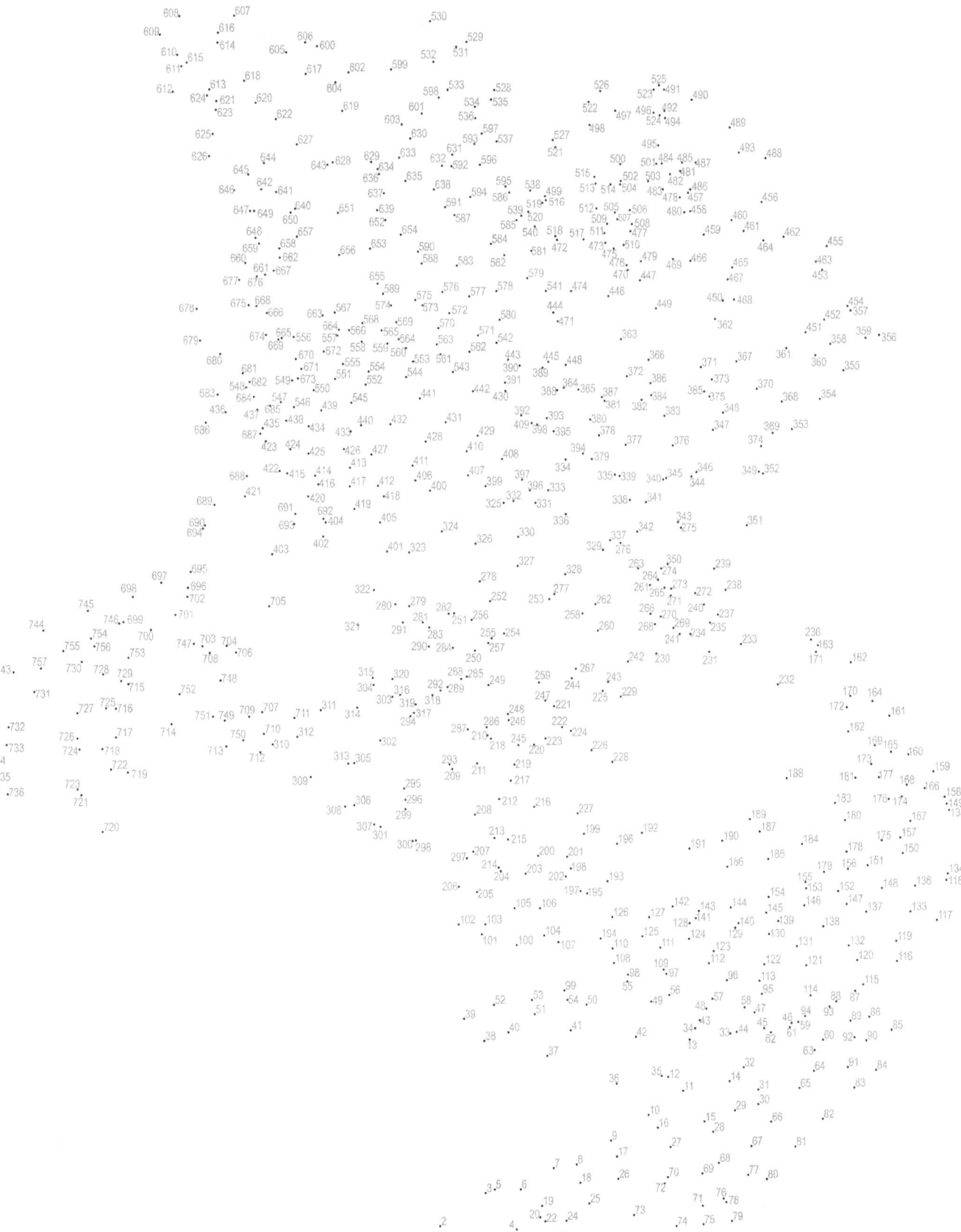

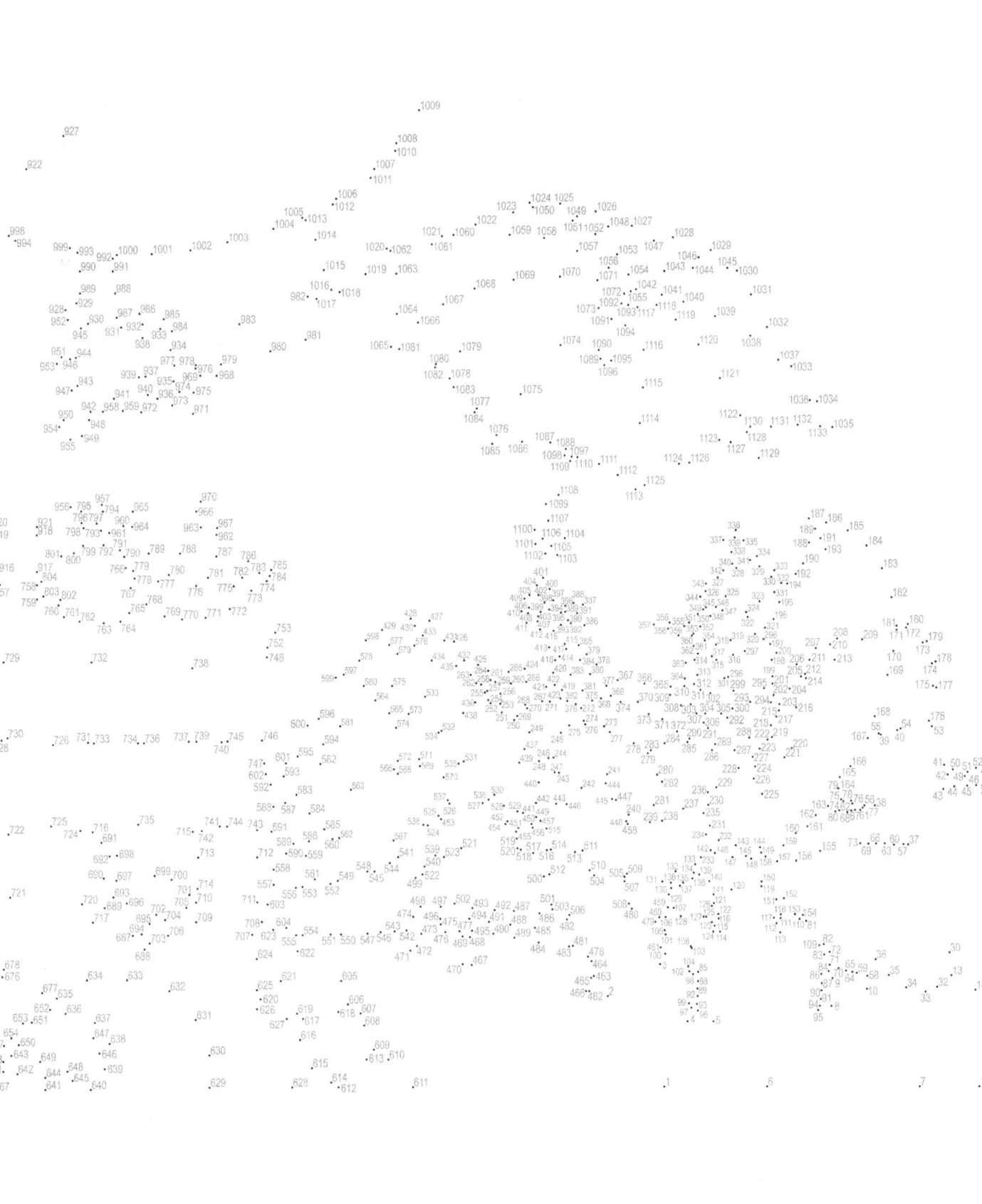

SOLUTIONS

Page 3: Mona Lisa – Leonardo da Vinci

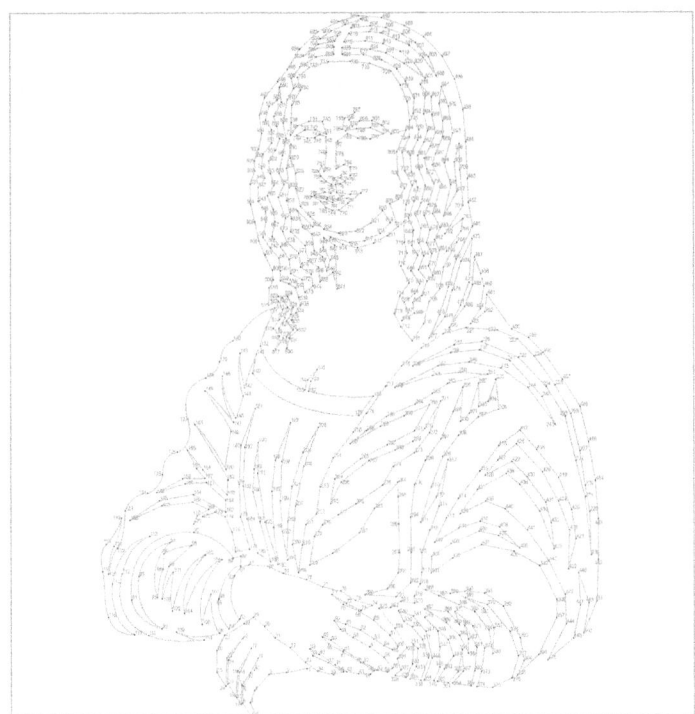

Page 5: Girl with a Pearl Earring – Johannes Vermeer

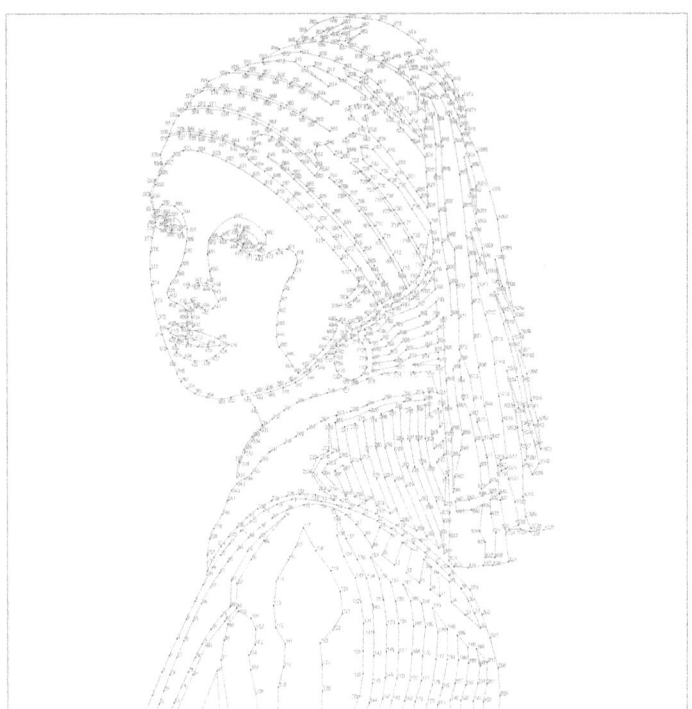

Page 7: Madonna in the Meadow – Raphael

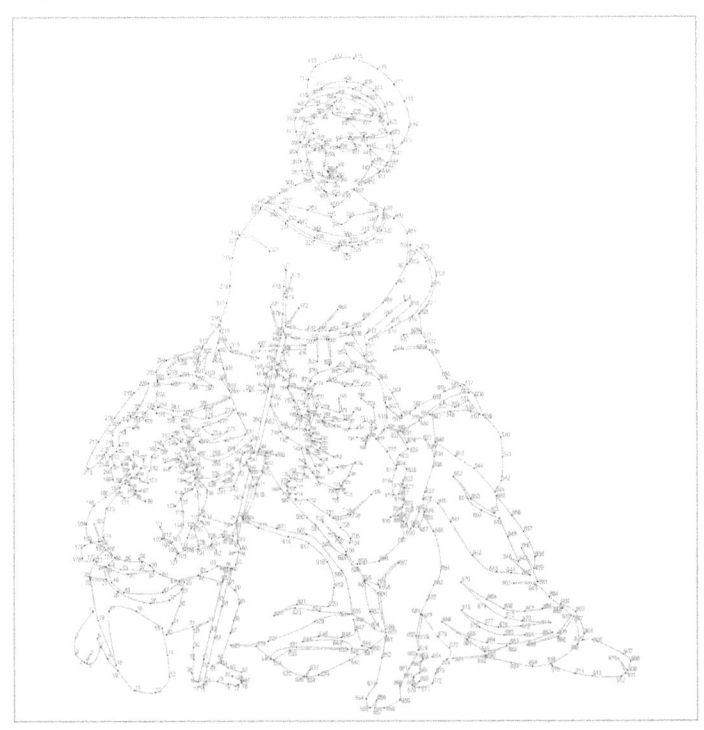

Page 9: Sunflowers – Vincent van Gogh

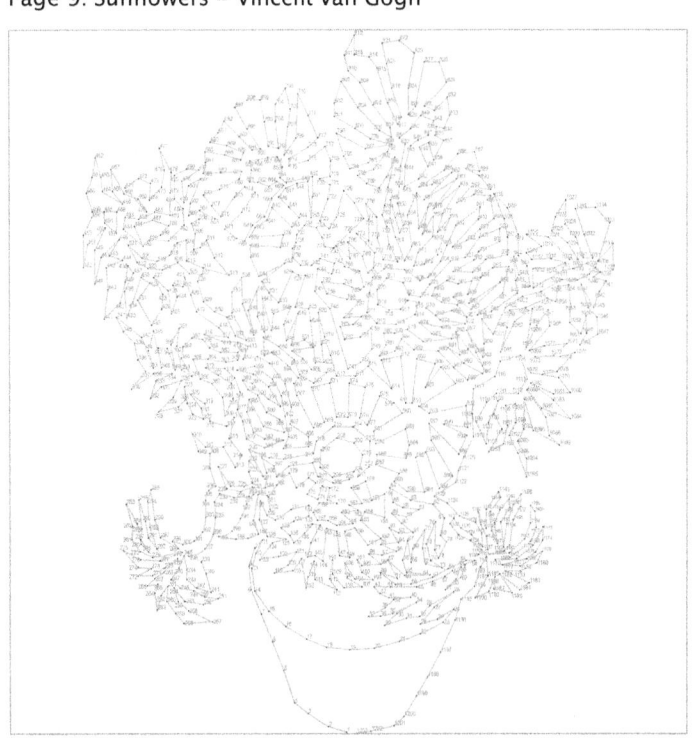

SOLUTIONS

Page 11: Café Terrace at Night – Vincent van Gogh

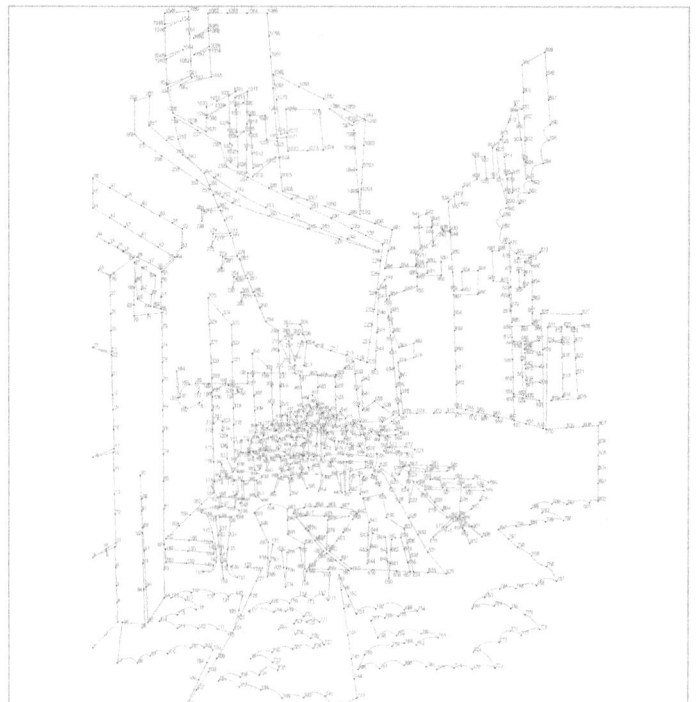

Page 13: Green Violinist – Marc Chagall

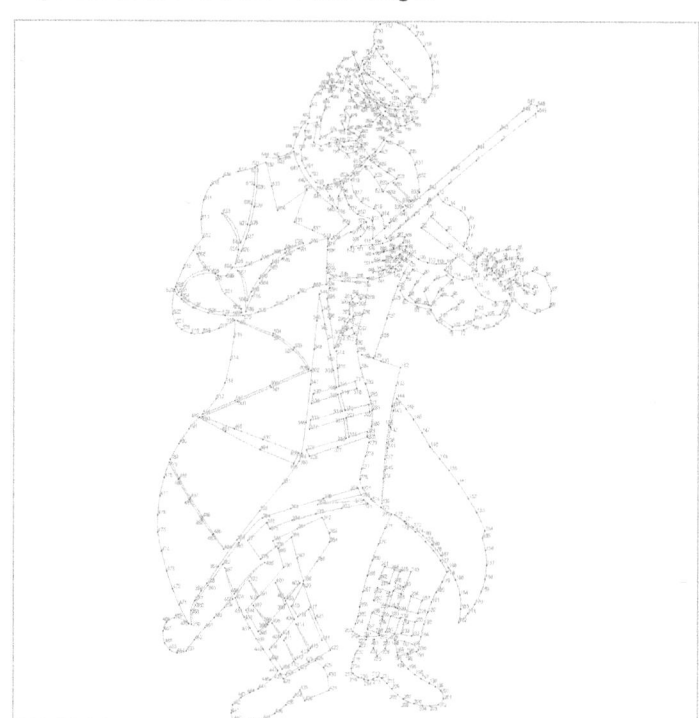

Page 15: David of Michelangelo

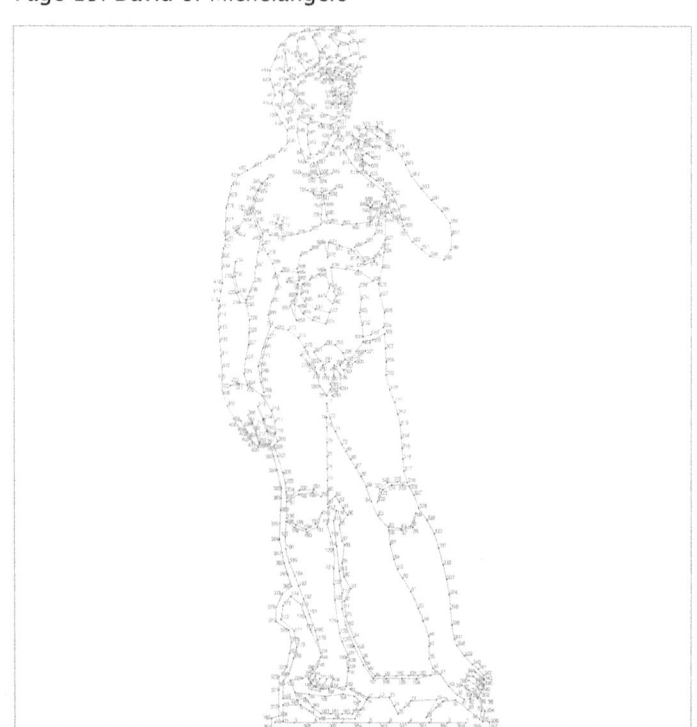

Page 17: Nefertiti Bust

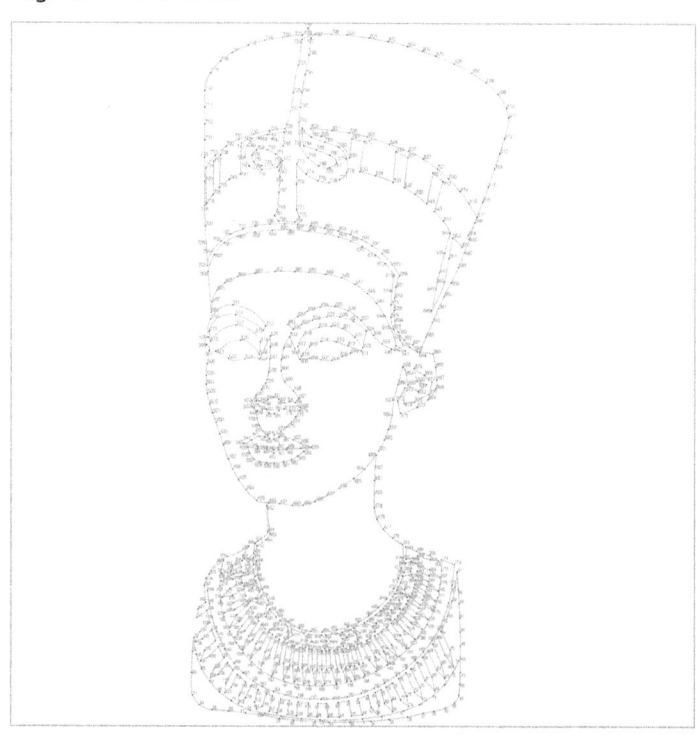

SOLUTIONS

Page 19: Winged Victory of Samothrace

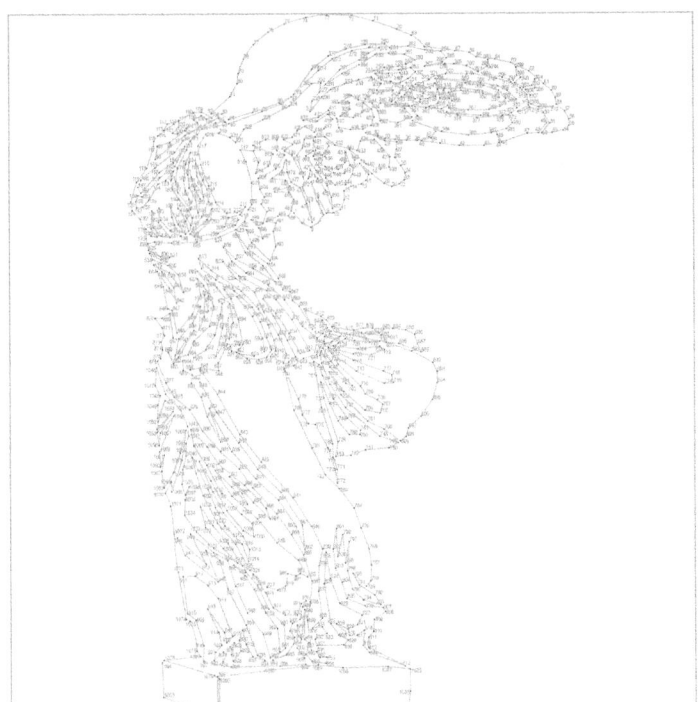

Page 21: Venus de Milo – Alexandros of Antioch

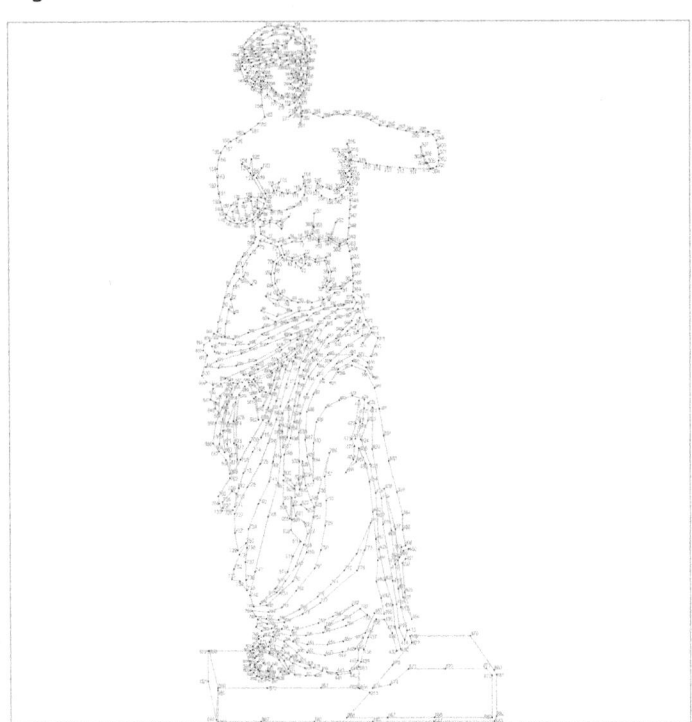

Page 23: Pietà – Michelangelo

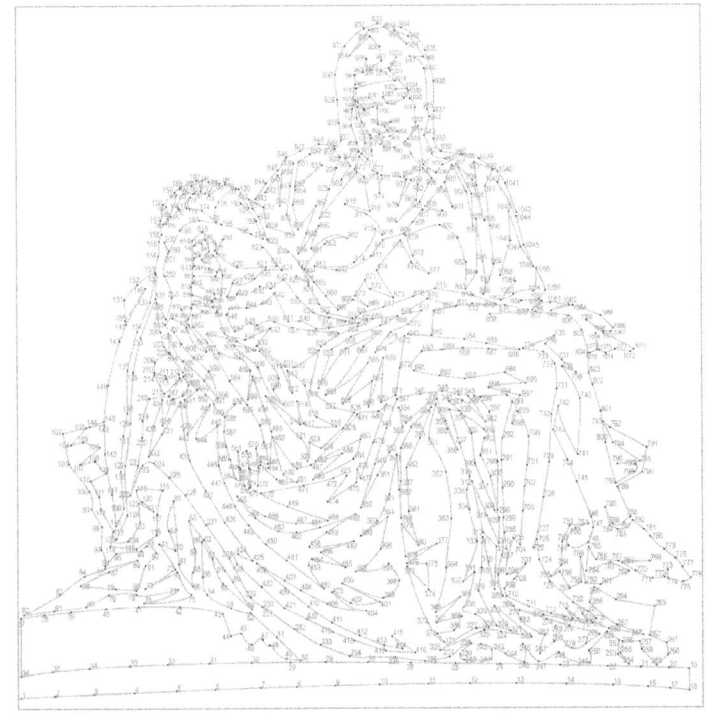

Page 25: Le Coq – Joan Miro

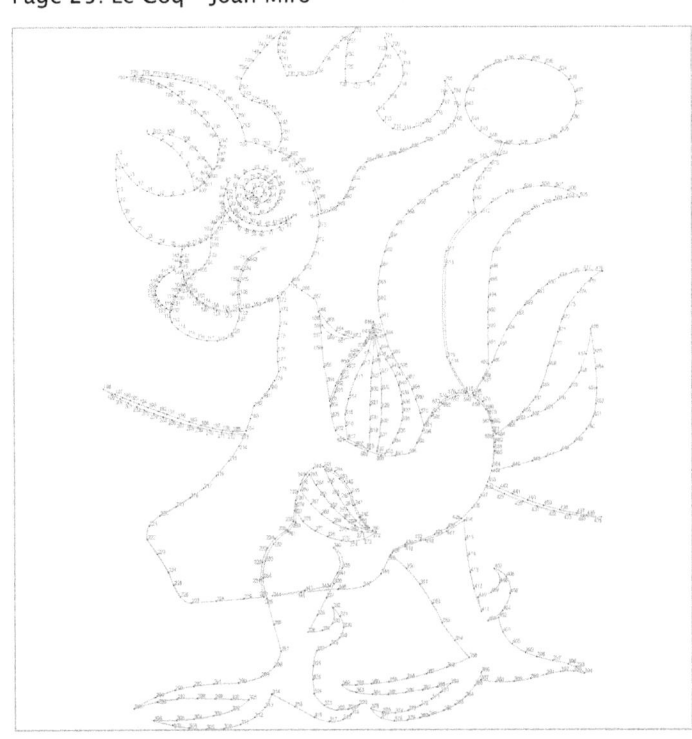

SOLUTIONS

Page 27: Nighthawks – Edward Hopper

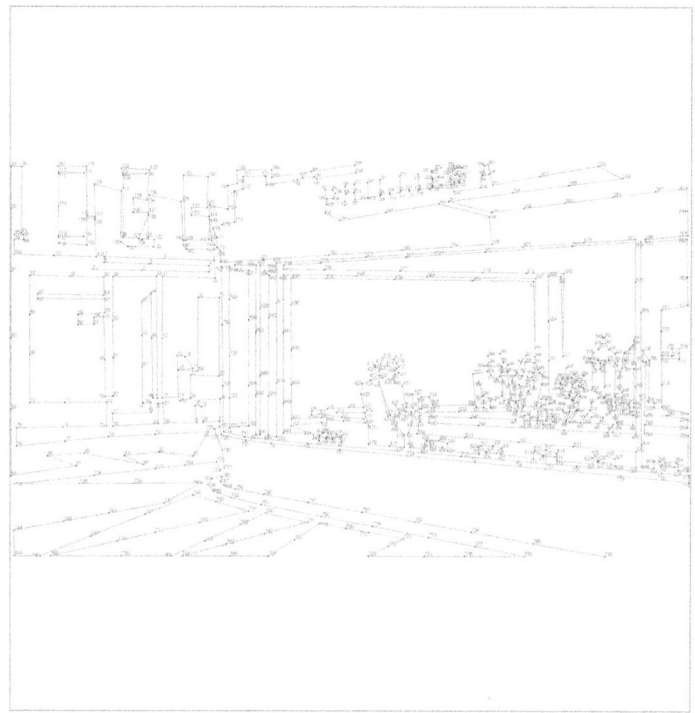

Page 29: Lady with an Ermine – Leonardo da Vinci

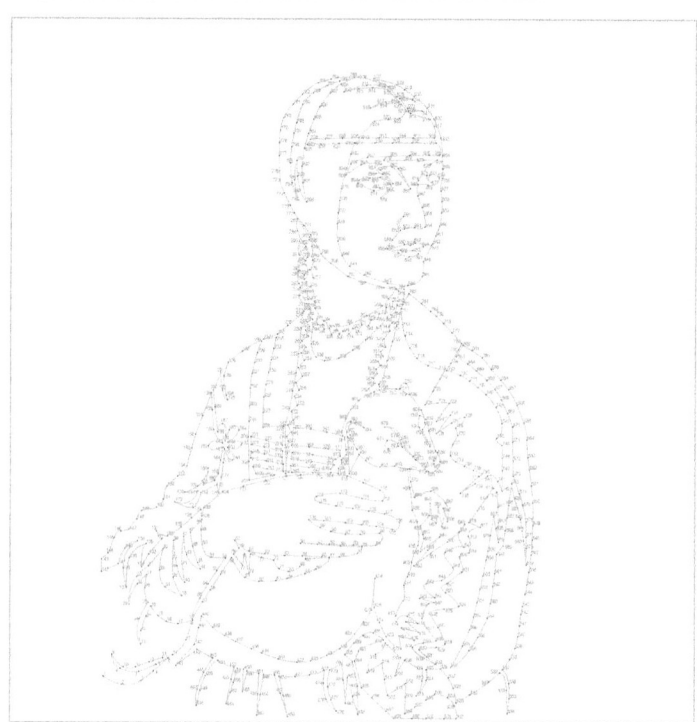

Page 31: Napoleon Crossing the Alps – Jacques-Louis DavidJacques-Louis David

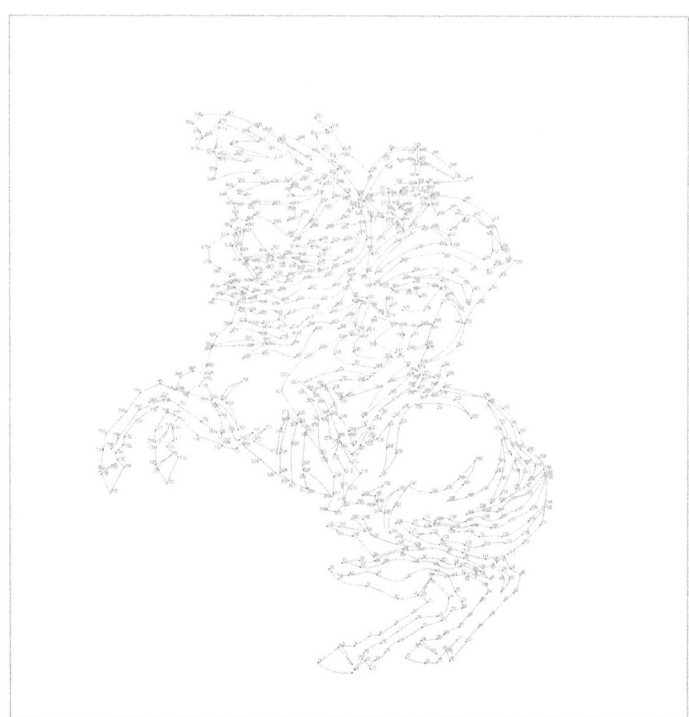

Page 33: The Poor Poet – Carl Spitzweg

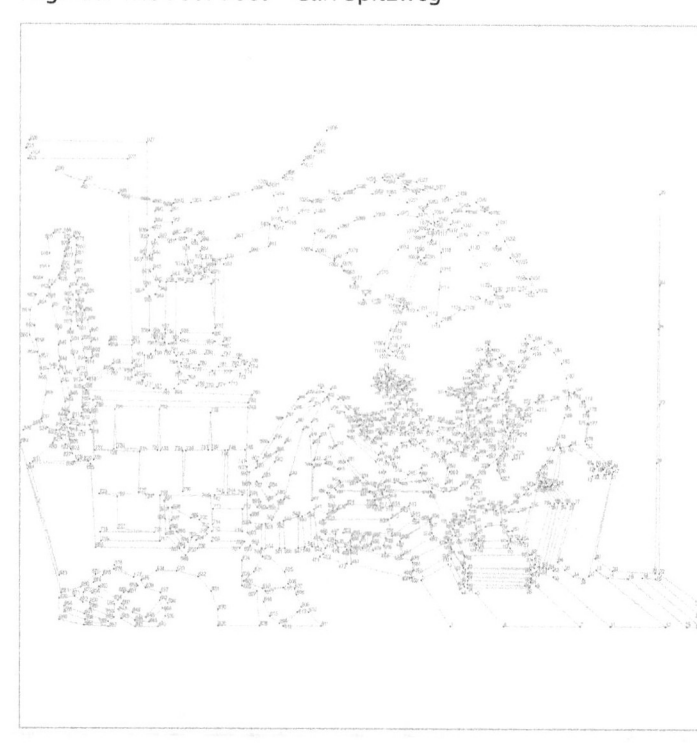

SOLUTIONS

Page 35: Temple Gardens – Paul Klee

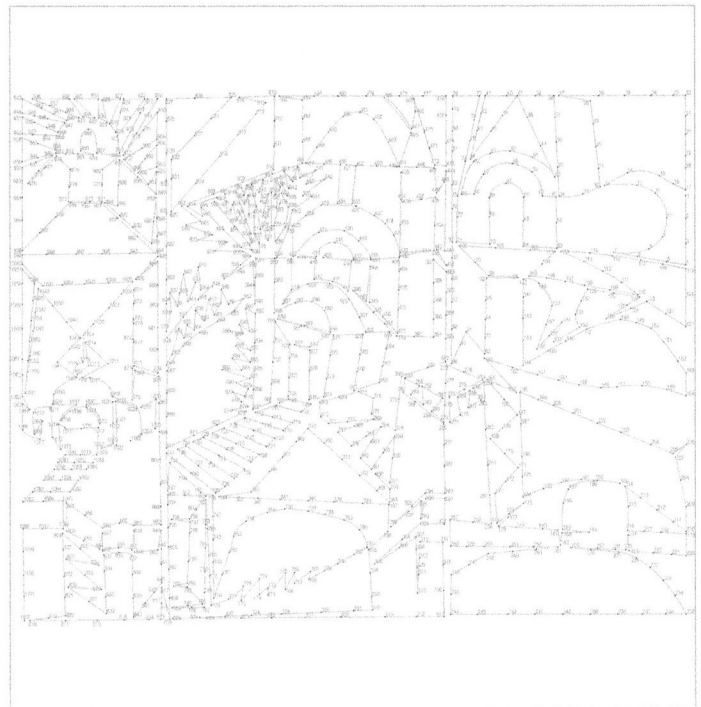

Page 37: Tahitian Women on the Beach – Paul Gauguinv

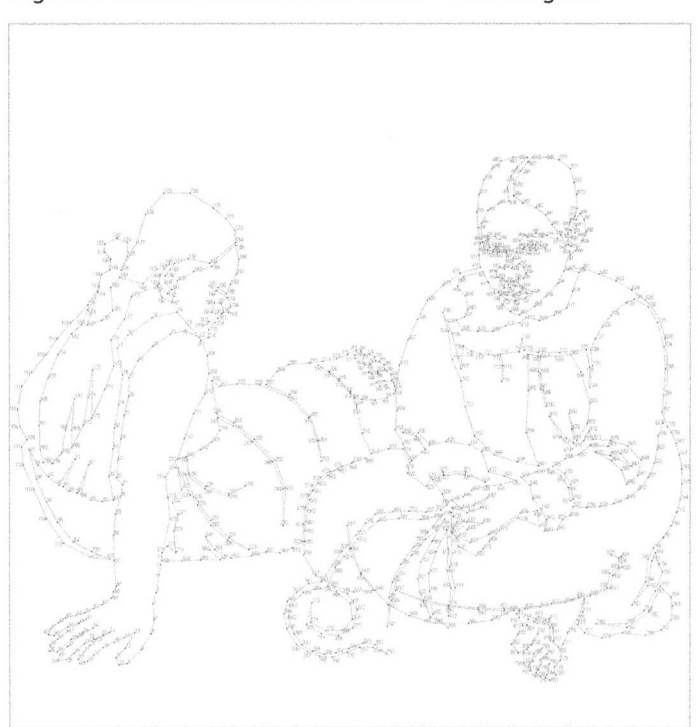

Page 39: Portrait of Marie–Thérèse Walter – Pablo Picasso

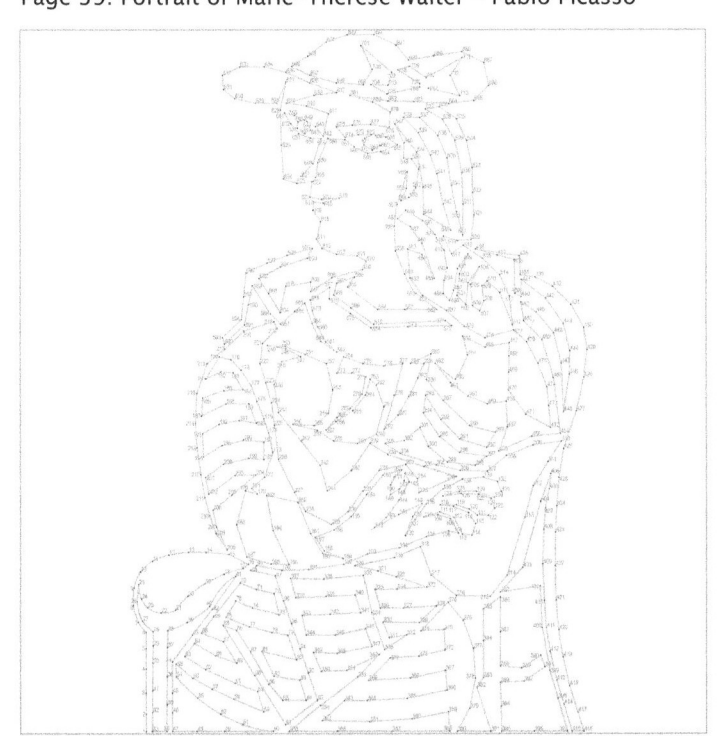

Page 41: American Gothic – Grant Wood

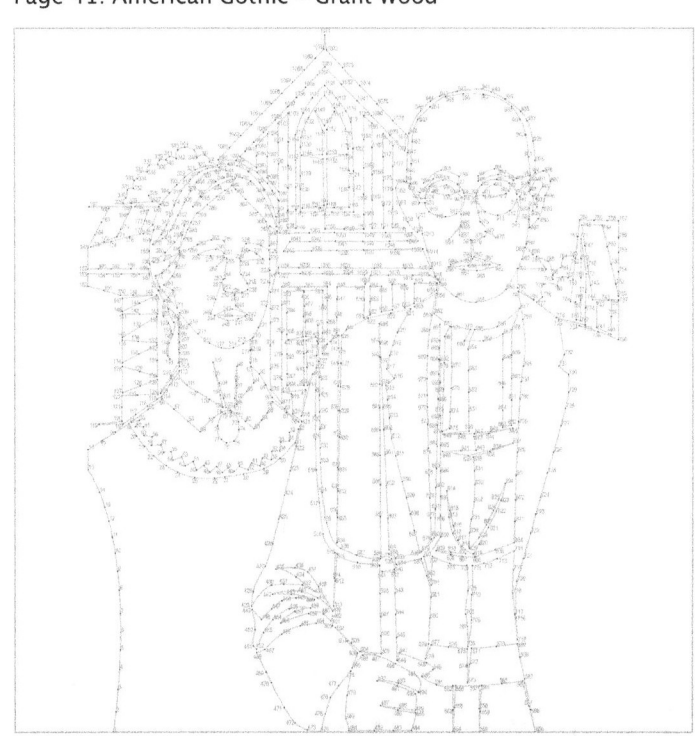